Bella & Emma,
You are fearfully & wonderfully
made.

✶ Achelle Bruce

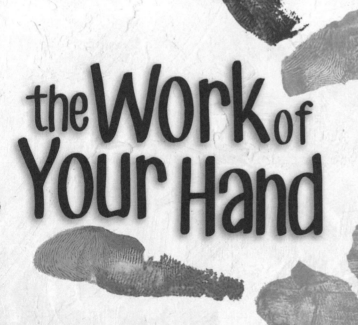

the Work of Your Hand

Fingerprints, GOD, and YOU!

by JENNIFER HALL RIVERA, EdD

Illustrated by
Hannah Jayne Lewin

First printing: January 2019

Copyright © 2019 by Jennifer Rivera. All rights reserved. No part of this book may be used or reproduced in any manner whatsoever without written permission of the publisher, except in the case of brief quotations in articles and reviews. For information write:
Master Books®, P.O. Box 726, Green Forest, AR 72638
Master Books® is a division of the New Leaf Publishing Group, Inc.

ISBN: 978-1-68344-157-1
ISBN: 978-1-61458-699-9 (digital)
Library of Congress Number: 2018966096

Illustrated by Hannah Jayne Lewin

Please consider requesting that a copy of this volume be purchased by your local library system.

Printed in the United States of America

Please visit our website for other great titles:
www.masterbooks.com

For information regarding author interviews,
please contact the publicity department at (870) 438-5288.

Master Books®
A Division of New Leaf Publishing Group
www.masterbooks.com

For downloadable copies of
this activity section, visit
masterbooks.com/free-downloads

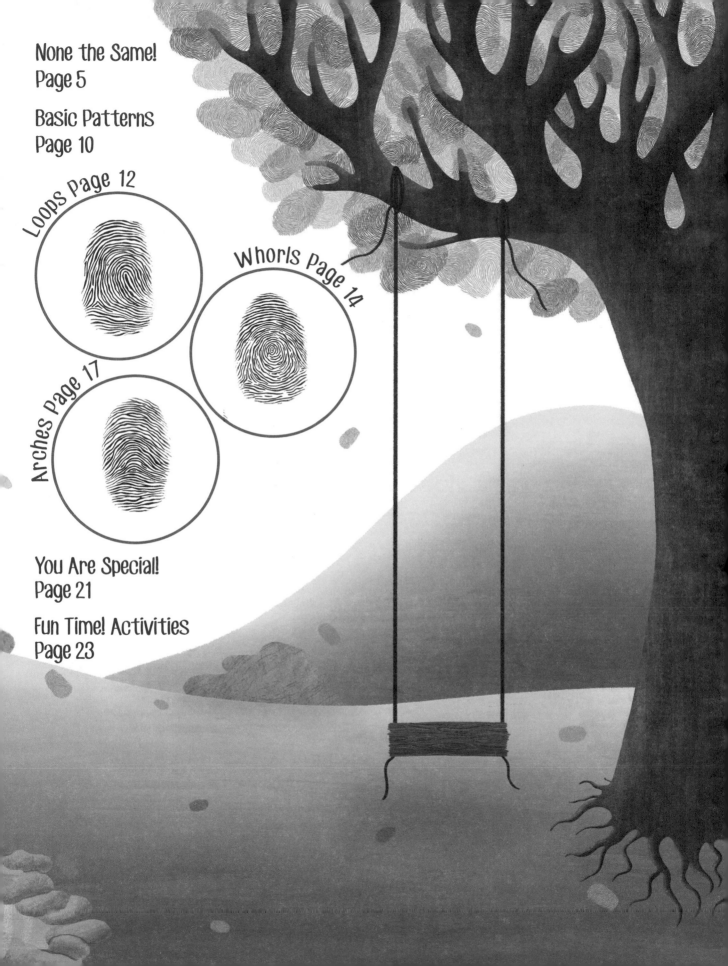

DEDICATION

This book is dedicated to my father, whose
expertise and passion for dactyloscopy inspired my
life-long interest in the field of forensic science.

Fearfully and wonderfully made are you,

For the Bible tells us this, and we know it is true.

The Bible can be trusted from cover to cover,

For it is spoken by God; above Him is no other.

God created you with a feature only you get.

A unique set of fingerprints uniquely set!

Fingerprints are found on you and me.
They are very easy to find as you will see.

7

Everyone's fingerprints differ in design.

Each finger is unique, and that is just fine!

Friction ridge skin found on hands and feet

Make your prints special and really neat.

What is friction ridge skin? God designed us with a unique skin on our hands and feet called "friction ridge skin." This skin is raised to create a non-slip surface. Take a look at the bottom of your sneakers. What do you see? Ridges! Sneaker makers copied God's perfect design and put non-slip ridges on the bottom of shoes just like on your hands and feet.

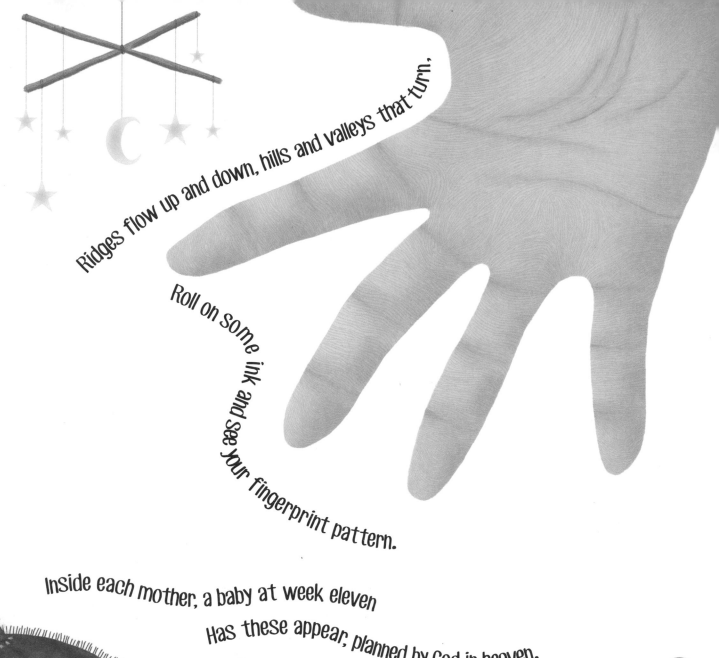

Ridges flow up and down, hills and valleys that turn.

Roll on some ink and see your fingerprint pattern.

Inside each mother, a baby at week eleven

Has these appear, planned by God in heaven.

The patterns' minutiae you find.
Make fingerprints one of a kind!

Arch

Loop

Whorl

1. Ridge Ending
2. Enclosure
3. Bifurcation
4. Island

Find little things!

Minutiae (my-NU-sha) is a big word for tiny things in your friction ridge skin that are unique to you.

The most common types:

1. **Ridge Ending:** Where the ridge ends

2. **Enclosure:** Looks like a thin circle

3. **Bifurcation:** Where a ridge becomes two or more

4. **Island:** Looks like a little island

These little details found in each fingerprint

Are special features that make you different.

YOU are special!

YOU are pawsome!

11

Now we will take a look at each pattern separately.

See if you can identify your fingerprint patterns correctly.

Loops look like a slide; it's rolling up and down fun!

Loops are most common; do you think you have one!

Radial and Ulnar are the two types of loops.
Named for bones in your arm, what a unique group!

Radius

Ulna

Let's stop and take a look at your prints!
Do you see any loops; do you need a hint?

Radial

Ulnar

65 percent of all fingerprints are a loop pattern.

Test yours here

Shaped like pinwheels, whorls do a swirl,

Like the center of a hurricane twirl!

There are whorls called plain,

double loop, and two more.

Central pocket and accidental are the last of the four!

The plain whorl is a pattern with a twirl.

Just like a yummy cinnamon bun swirl.

Double loop whorls, what shape would you guess?

Just look for two curves in the shape of S.

Tiny and light, like a snail's little shell,

A central pocket loop whorl is easy to tell.

The final whorl pattern is an accidental.
Not for a mistake, but for being original.

Let's stop for a moment to look at your prints.
Do you see any whorls; do you need any hints?

Plain Whorl

**Central Pocket
Loop Whorl**

**Double Loop
Whorl**

Accidental Whorl

Test yours here

**Accidental Whorls are no accident! It is a combination of two or more patterns with
the exception of a plain arch. They are very rare and are only 1% of all whorl patterns.**

The last type of fingerprint is the most rare,
The arch is hard to see so be very aware.

The arch is named either plain or tented;
On your fingers, is an arch represented?

Uphill and downhill; see how it goes!

Like a rolling hill, the plain arch flows,

Just like a teepee, its frame is slanting.

Tented arches remind us of camping,

Let's stop for a minute to look at your prints.
Do you see any arches; do you need hints?

Plain Arch

Tented Arch

5 percent of all fingerprints are an Arch pattern.

Test yours here

You have learned about Arches, Loops, and Whorls.
Which look a lot like slides, tents, hills, and swirls.

20 unique patterns are found on your hands and your feet.
God's design for prints are pretty awesome and neat.

God made you special with unique design.
Thank Him today for His creations are divine.

Fearfully and wonderfully made are you,
For the Bible tells us this,
and we know it is true.

You can have more fun using your fingertips,
And make a variety of designs using these hints.

I praise you, for I am fearfully and wonderfully made.
Wonderful are your works; my soul knows it very well.
Psalm 139:14

God Loves You! Use your fingerprints to fill in the heart below.

For downloadable copies of this activity section, visit **masterbooks.com/free-downloads**

I will give thanks
to the LORD
with my whole heart...
Psalm 9:1

Place two of your fingerprints together like this to make another heart in the box!

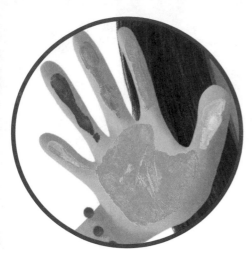

Show Your Hand! Use finger paints or finger ink pads to put colors on your fingers and the center of your hand. Use as many as you want! Press down on the paper below to make a colorful handprint.

So God created man in his own image,
in the image of God he created him;
male and female he created them.
Genesis 1:27

Flowerprint! Did you know God created flowers on Day 3?

See the pretty picture of the fingerprint flower in the box? Now it's time to make your own 'flowerprint' below! Choose different colors to add petals and leaves.

The earth brought forth vegetation, plants yielding seed according to their own kinds, and trees bearing fruit in which is their seed, each according to its kind. And God saw that it was good. And there was evening and there was morning, the third day.

Genesis 1:12-13

1, 2, 3 - Animal Art! Let's make some fingerprint animals! See if you can use the following examples to make your own animal art. Hint! Be sure to use the same number of fingerprints that each example used.

One thumb print

Two thumb prints

Three thumb prints

26

Make a Leaf! It's time to make a fingerprint leaf in the blank space below.

1. Make a fingerprint.

2. Draw a line on it.

3. Add extra lines.

You're done! There is room to make more
if you want – use different fingers and colors!

A Caterpillar! You will need to use two different colors to make this one!.

1. Put three
fingerprints here.
Leave space between.

2. Add two fingerprints
in a different color
like this.

3. Add lines for feet
and the happy face!

 Be A Busy Bee! You can use colorful fingerprints to complete the animals below like this bee! Some may take more than one fingerprint to complete. Have fun!

 Funny Fingerprint Faces! Use your fingerprints to complete the funny faces below.

Colors For The Seasons! God created the sun and moon to separate light from dark and for seasons on Day 4 of the creation week. All these trees are missing leaves, and your fingerprints make great ones! Make sure to change colors for each tree to represent the changing colors of the seasons.

Spring is when everything is bright green and new with a few leaves showing up here and there on the branches, some bigger and some smaller.

Summer shows the many colors of green all around us and the trees are covered with many, many leaves.

Fall is the most colorful time for trees when their leaves are colored in greens, yellows, oranges, reds, and the colors in between! Be sure to use different colors.

And God said, Let there be lights in the expanse of the heavens to separate the day from the night. And let them be for signs and for seasons, and for days and years.
Genesis 1:14

Winter means only a few leaves are left on the tree with some laying on the ground. Most of these leaves will be different colors of brown and tan.

 A Fingerprint Zoo! God created flying creatures and sea creatures on Day 5 and land animals on Day 6 of the creation week. Complete the animal faces below and discover all the animals!

And God said, 'Let the waters swarm with swarms of living creatures, and let birds fly above the earth across the expanse of the heavens'. And there was evening and there was morning, the fifth day.'

Genesis 1:20, 23

 How Many To Finish? God created land animals on Day 6! There are a lot of animals below that need to be fingerprint finished! Some will take one fingerprint to complete. Others will take more fingerprints. Have fun completing in this fingerprint zoo!

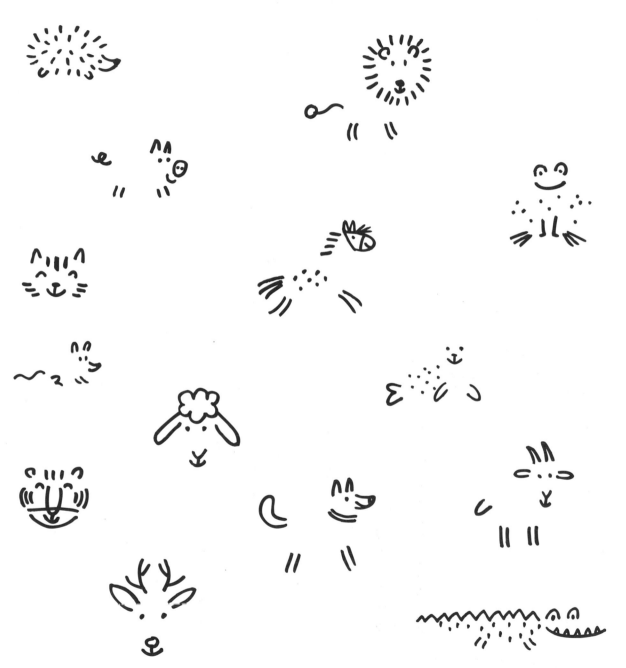

'And God made the beasts of the earth according to their kinds and the livestock according to their kinds, and everything that creeps on the ground according to its kind.' ...And there was evening and there was morning, the sixth day.'

Genesis 1:25,31

Welcome To Fingerprint City! Things are a little boring in Fingerprint City. Add your fingerprints to the image below to make Fingerprint City a colorful, fun place!

A World of Wheels! Fingerprint City is missing many vehicles for people to use. Help them by finishing the fingerprint vehicles below, and see how many fun ways people will have to move around their city!

A Big Design! Just like God created you with fingerprints all your own, God made the world and creatures around us. This includes the spiders who make beautiful webs. Use your fingerprints to finish the spiders below.

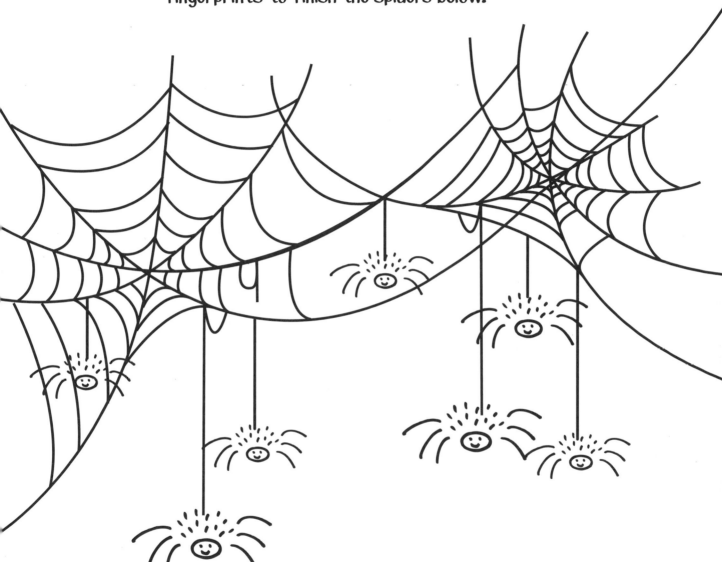

O LORD, how manifold are your works!
In wisdom have you made them all; the earth is full of your creatures.
Psalm 104:24

Stand Still Little Feet! When you were born, the doctor may have put your footprints on your birth certificate. Now let's see if you can create a pair of footprints here. You will need your parent to help you get the fingerprint ink on your feet and help to put the paper on the floor. Then, sit in a chair and press your footprints to this page. Be sure to clean off your feet when you are done!

Funny Footprint! Remember when the book talked about special skin with ridges on your hands and feet? Let's see what your footprint looks like and we will discover your shoe size at the same time! Put your fingerprint paint or ink on your right foot and then place your foot on the image here.

Make sure to clean off your foot after this activity!

Ponder the path of your feet;
then all your ways will be sure.
Proverbs 4:26

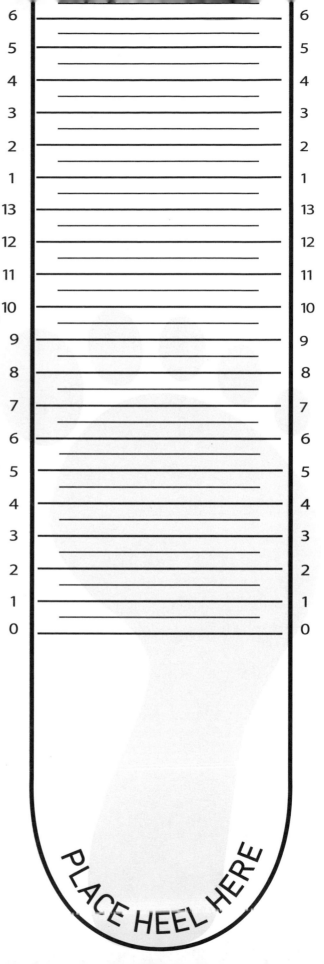

PLACE HEEL HERE

Berry Baskets! It's time to pick berries, and you need to get the correct number of berries for each basket. Use your fingerprints to add fingerprint berries. Use as many fun colors as you want!

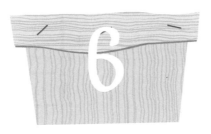

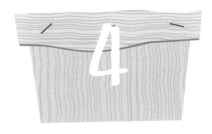

A Bunch of Balloons! It's a beautiful day to play with balloons, but we don't have any. Use your fingerprints to add fingerprint balloons to the strings and create a colorful picture!

My Fingerprint Record! Choose your favorite color and make a complete record of your fingerprints. Put a fingerprint of each finger in the boxes below.

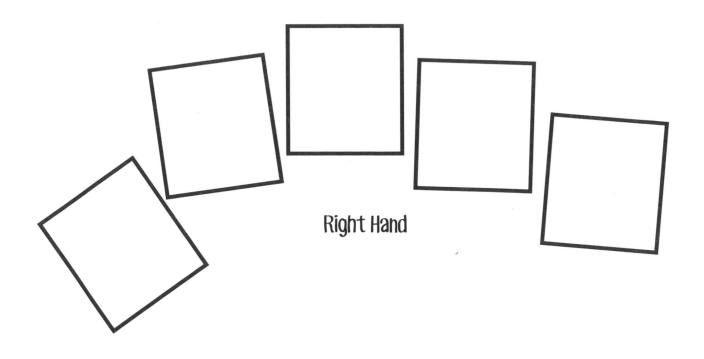

Right Hand

Wow, you have amazing fingerprints!

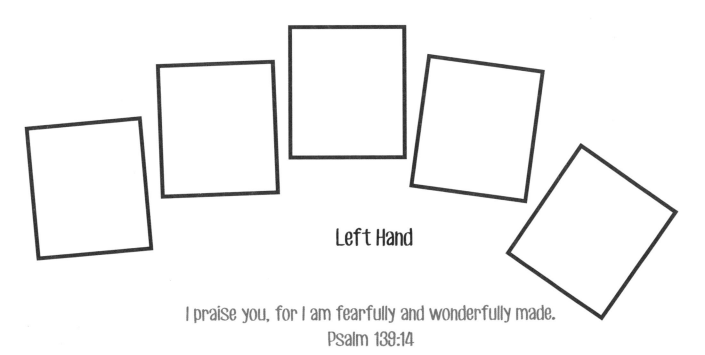

Left Hand

I praise you, for I am fearfully and wonderfully made.
Psalm 139:14

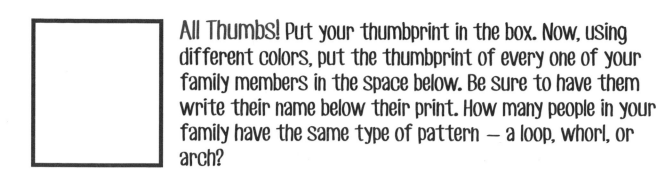

All Thumbs! Put your thumbprint in the box. Now, using different colors, put the thumbprint of every one of your family members in the space below. Be sure to have them write their name below their print. How many people in your family have the same type of pattern — a loop, whorl, or arch?

Creation Week! God created all the world and the universe during the six days of creation. See if you can use your fingerprints to finish the pictures below for each day of the Creation Week.

Day 1

Light and earth

Day 2

Separation of waters

Day 3

Dry land
and plants

  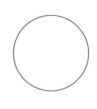

Day 4

Sun, moon, planets and stars

Day 5

Flying and sea creatures

Day 6

Land animals
and man

Use your fingerprints to remind you of the Savior!
Choose one or more colors, and fill in the cross below with your fingerprints.

"For God so loved the world, that he gave his only Son, that whoever
believes in him should not perish but have eternal life.

John 3:16

Jennifer Hall Rivera, EdD, is the Education Specialist at the Creation Museum, where she presents daily workshops and develops children's educational programs. Her interest in the forensic sciences started at an early age and is credited to the godly instruction of her father, a renowned fingerprint expert. Her experience in the field of forensic science includes employment in a crime scene unit, over a decade of teaching, journal publications, and numerous speaking events. Dr. Rivera is excited to present fingerprint science for children through the lens of God's Word.

For more information about Dr. Rivera's workshops and other events at the Creation Museum, visit www. creationmuseum.org/events/workshops/

THINK
BIGGER

Plan your visit at ArkEncounter.com

Williamstown, KY
(south of Cincinnati)